Counting Snowflakes

Counting Book For Children
Coloring Book Included

Brenda J. Sullivan
Kathryn A. Sullivan

Counting Snowflakes

ISBN: 978-1-7329990-2-2

Published by Tree Roots Press

Photography
Aaron Burden - Upsplash
Google Images
Wikipedia
Brenda J. Sullivan
Artwork
Brenda J. Sullivan
Kathryn A. Sullivan

Requests to publish work from this book should be sent to:
Treerootspress@gmail.com
brenda@brendajsullivanbooks.com

Tree Roots Press

treerootspress.com

Dedicated to all who love to explore nature!

Picture of a real snowflake

Katie with Mommy being silly while we paint

Katie with Daddy on one of our beach walks

Katie finishing up one of her whale pictures. Yes, we paint outside the lines!

Meet the Artist!

Katie

Katie is a wheelchair-bound young lady with severe cerebral palsy and epilepsy among many other medical problems. She is also nonverbal with very limited vision. Despite these challenges, she has a fighting spirit and has learned how to use basic communication skills and assistive technology to produce various arts and craft products.

This is one of Katie's "Able Gifts" – a product she's helped create with her Mother, Brenda J. Sullivan, when she is in good health and "able" to do so. Proceeds from these books are used to support the costs of Katie's craft-works and enable her to more fully engage her world.

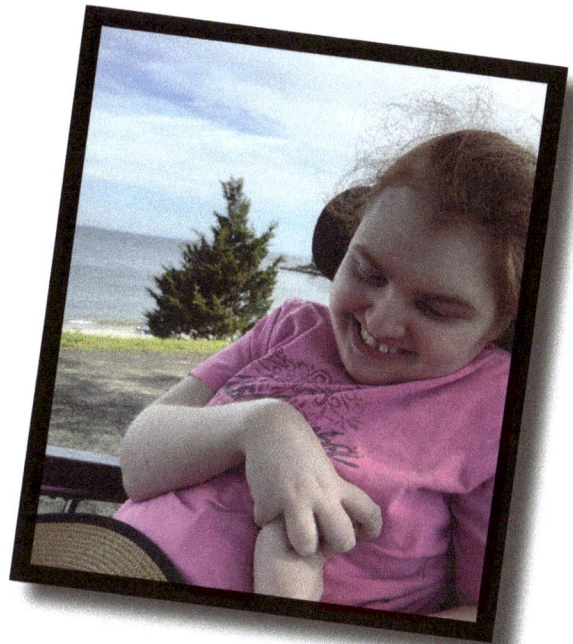

Katie is excited when a whale swims by the window at the sea aquarium

1

One Snowflake

2

Two Snowflakes

3

Three Snowflakes

4

Four Snowflakes

5

Five Snowflakes

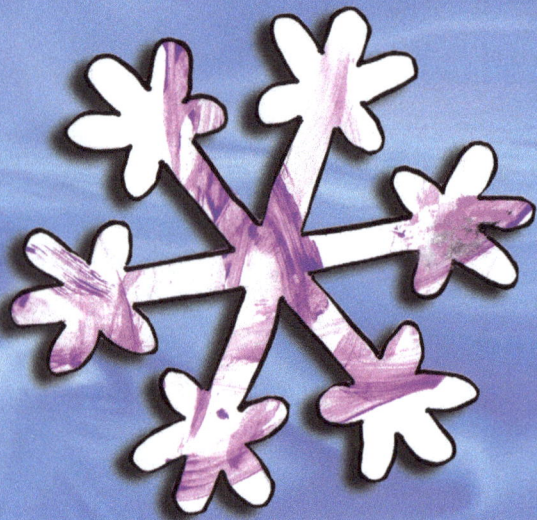

6

Six Snowflakes

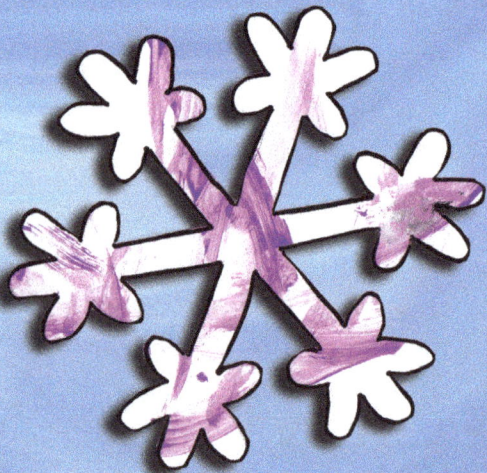

7

Seven Snowflakes

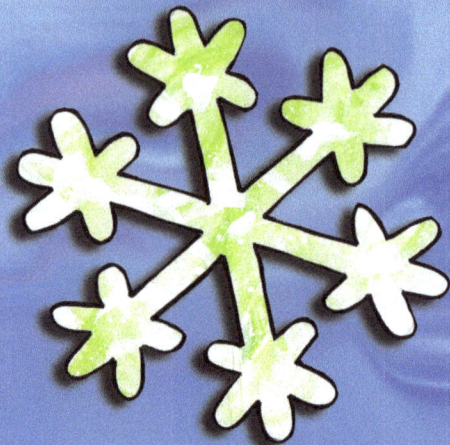

8

Eight Snowflakes

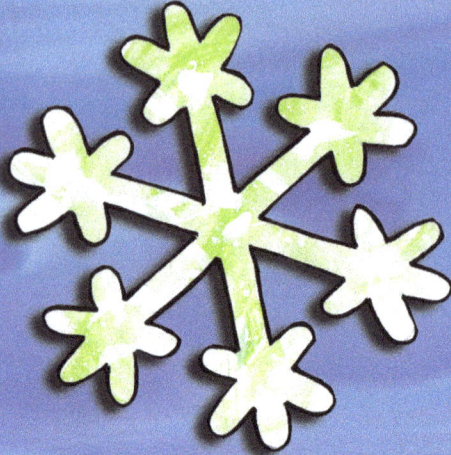

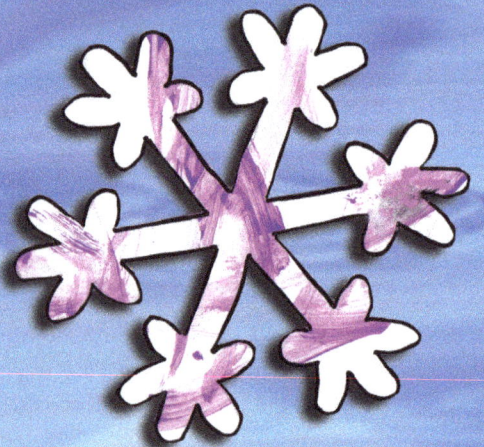

9

Nine Snowflakes

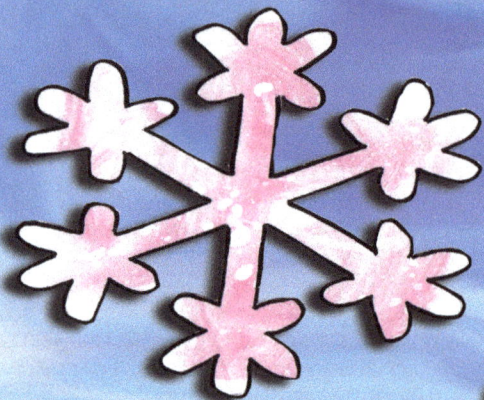

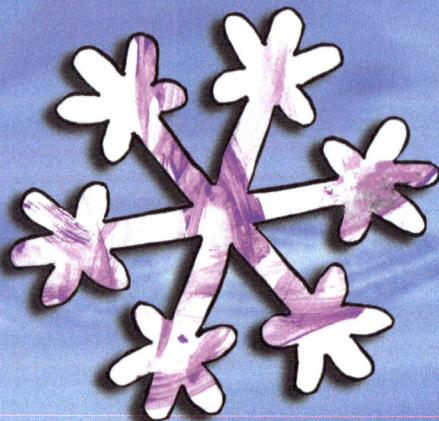

10

Ten Snowflakes

Photographs of real snowflakes

Wilson Bentley's Snowflakes

Wilson Bentley first person to photograph snowflakes

Every snowflake in nature is different

Fun Facts About Snowflakes

- Wilson Bentley was the first known person to photograph snowflakes in 1885 – over 135 years ago. He figured out how to mount a camera onto a microscope and take pictures of snowflakes on black velvet fabric.

- A snowflake is a cold-water droplet that freezes on a dust particle and falls to the ground. As it falls, it goes through different temperatures and humidity zones. As it gets closer, it changes its shape and detail.

- In 1951, scientists from the International Association of Cryospheric Sciences created a classification system that characterized snowflakes into ten basic shapes.

- The shapes include the stellar crystals (i.e., the style of snowflake picked for this book) are the most commonly recognized than the irregular shaped snowflakes forms such as capped columns. This system is still used today, and over the years have added more complex forms.

- Warm and wet conditions in the air make the best detailed snowflakes. In comparison, drier, colder conditions make flatter, less complicated flakes.

1

One Snowflake

2

Two Snowflakes

3

Three Snowflakes

4

Four Snowflakes

5

Five Snowflakes

6

Six Snowflakes

7
Seven Snowflakes

8

Eight Snowflakes

9

Nine Snowflakes

10
Ten Snowflakes

About Our Family

Brenda Sullivan lives in South Glastonbury, CT with her husband Paul and their daughter Katie.

They are avid nature lovers and gardeners who took their love of gardening to a new level by converting their 1.3 acres into a small farm called Thompson Street Farm LLC.

Brenda is an herbalist and market gardener who specializes in growing lavender, medicinal herbs and flowers. She also makes handcrafted goat's milk herbal soaps and herbal bath products using the herbs, flowers, fruits and vegetables grown on their farm or purchased from other local farmers.

More information on her bath and body products can be found at www.farmtobath.com

Katie, the love of their life and the center of their universe, has a number of serious medical conditions including severe cerebral palsy, epilepsy and very limited vision. She is nonverbal and wheelchair bound but these challenges have not prevented Katie from experiencing life.

Katie experiences the world on her terms with the help of assistive technology, other sensory, adaptations and years of homeschooling experience. Katie understands basic concepts and has developed many interests including an appreciation for music, painting with her Mother, and listening to stories.

She loves being outdoors and we've discovered that enabling her to experience the natural world has been Katie's best educator. This has been our inspiration for creating nature themed children's books.

Connect with Brenda online:
www.brendajsullivanbooks.com
www.thompsonstreetfarm.com
www.farmtobath.com
www.livingandlovinherbs.com
Facebook.com/brendajsullivanbooks
Facebook.com/livingandlovinherbspodcast

Other Books By Brenda J. Sullivan

Children's Books

Counting Starfish
Counting Book For Children
Coloring Book Included
2nd Edition
Brenda J. Sullivan
Kathryn A. Sullivan

Counting Dragonflies
Counting Book For Toddlers
Coloring Book Included
Brenda J. Sullivan
Kathryn A. Sullivan

My Garden Journal
A "How To" Garden Book For Kids
By Brenda J. Sullivan and
Kathryn A. Sullivan

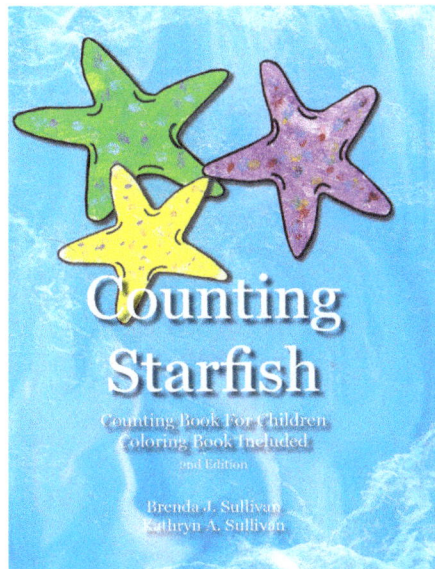

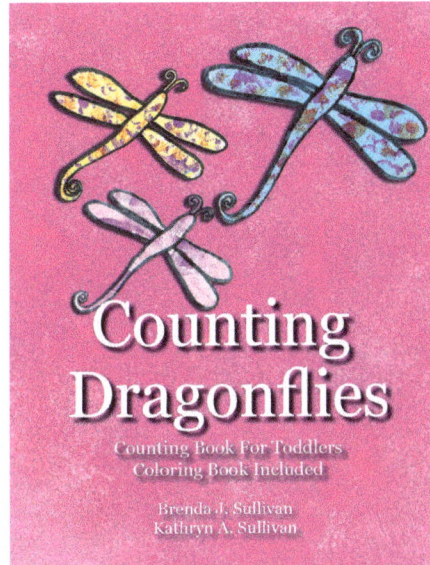

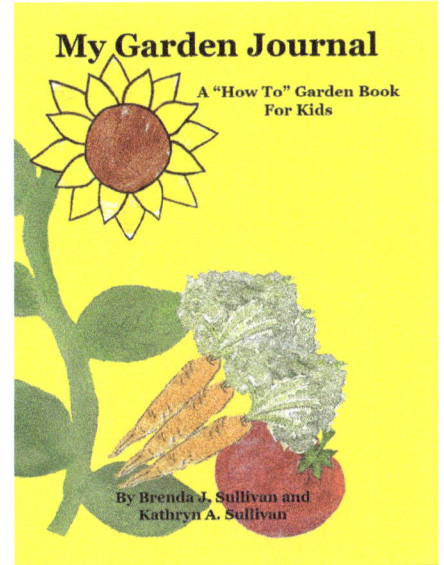

Available in all stores and libraries - just ask!

Journals

Lavender Journal Notebook

Lavender Journal Notebook Volume 2

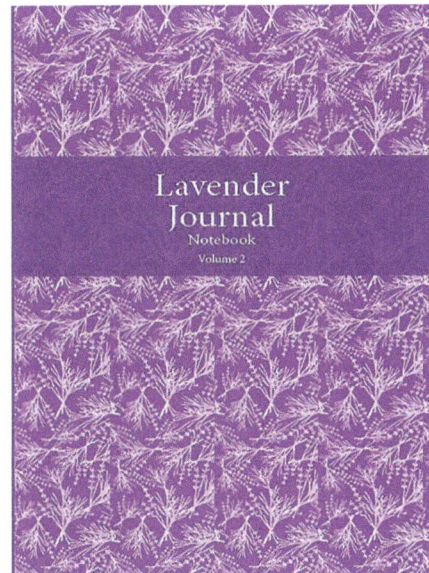

Available on Amazon

www.ingramcontent.com/pod-product-compliance
Lightning Source LLC
Chambersburg PA
CBHW042354030426
42336CB00029B/3484